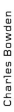

Charles Bowden

EUGENE
RICHARDS 55

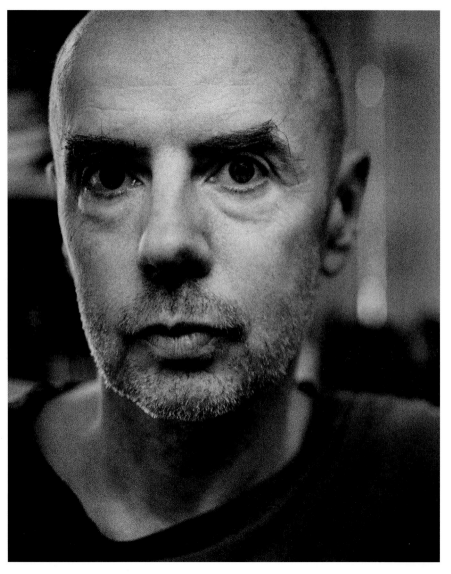

Gene Richards by John Morgan, 2000

2.3

He is the monk with wife, child and dog. Now grey light glides on the waxed wood floor of the three-storey Brooklyn house built at the end of the nineteenth century. Janine works a floor below doing the billings, Sam is off at school and Tom curls up by the back door, dreaming of sun and spring days. He sits on the sofa facing the white walls, his lap full of photographs, fifty-five photographs and they are arranged chronologically, and God, he says, he is fifty-five and for the first time in his life there is this summing up, and it is piled up on his lap, three decades of doing something with a camera. And now he is looking back, not through the aperture, not ahead, not around the cool clean room, but back. He's been on the edge of this country before. That time when Dorothea died and he thought of dying himself. That time when Janine told him she was carrying his child and she thought he might bolt right out the door. And this time, with all the years staring up from his lap with eyes of other faces.

The head is balding, hair close-cropped, the same with the beard. Attention lingers on the head, the head that was beaten until memory was destroyed and life almost ended. The eyes look carefully, always carefully, through thin-framed glasses. The eyes that saw things but needed a language and then found the camera. The body shambles, and unless one is very alert, almost disappears. Nondescript, that is the body, a form barely noticed. The body that went into the districts of crack and death. And of course, when the body seems to disappear, the camera becomes all but forgotten. Everything comes across low-key, relaxed. Even the voice is that way in the beginning, soft, purling along, just registering above a mumble. The hands move delicately, oh so carefully, the fingers touch the pile of material. And on the lap, in the grey light, the photographs, a volcano that has been erupting for thirty years and yet the fires are still not banked.

The first time I met Eugene Richards he said, 'People are always disappointed when they meet me. They expect more.' Sometimes they expect him to be a black man. Always they expect him to be a big, bruising, tough guy. He looked down at the floor of the hotel lobby as he said this.

He is looking straight ahead, not at me beside him on the sofa, but straight ahead. He is going back to the beginning, peeling off the years like scabs, trying to return, to imagine that beginning. At fifty-five he is no longer so sure just when and where it began, he simply knows that now he is in it, deep in and carried along by strong currents he cannot really name or control, and that this pile of photographs, this force propelling him, these black-and-white rectangles are his life and there is no escaping this fact. And that is where the importance of the waxed wood floor comes in, and also – and he says this softly – that terrible sound, that sound almost like a scream echoing off the walls of this room, a sound that rocks his life's work and makes him question everything piled up on his lap, and what he holds in his lap is the book you now hold in your lap, and he is saying – and God, that voice, so soft, almost flat, slow in cadence, a laconic voice at first, but then it begins moving, picking up speed like a locomotive leaving the station, the clickedy-clack of the rails increases in tempo, the voice surges, a harsh lyricism suddenly flowers out of the soft tones, and then, I can hear this scream, this awful scream – he is saying he can no longer abide the silence of photographs. That's really it: the walls are white, the wood underfoot gleams with polish, the silence of photographs. But first, the importance of the waxed wooden floor.

The hair a white crown over the glowing face, the words a strange language of sacred form, the name is Minor White and he becomes the bridge taken by Gene

Richards to a larger world. White is a handmaiden of photography, a link to the effort begun by Alfred Stieglitz to make the camera image a zone of art. From 1952 onward, White struggled forging Aperture, both the magazine and the institution. He lived on almost nothing, drank much, loved men, and fortified himself with the faiths of the Orient. He said things like, 'No matter what role we are in — photographer, beholder, critic — inducing silence for seeing in ourselves, we are given to see from a sacred place. From that place the sacredness of everything may be seen.'

Richards arrives in his early twenties. The Vietnam War rages, it is the late sixties, and Richards like most young men of his time is waiting to be devoured. He hails emotionally from Dorchester, an Irish, Polish, Italian enclave of Boston, a place of cheap flats for working people, corner taverns and too many grey days. It is a world where the eyes are wary and the advice is watch out. At twelve, the family moves to the suburbs, but it is a more spacious version of the city streets. The doors are always locked on the homes and the world is a set of cold compartments for Richards. The ceilings are always dropped, the floors hidden with linoleum and rugs, the furniture smothered by pillows, every surface cluttered with figurines and treasured glassware, the air fading into gloom. There is a snapshot of him as a boy, maybe taken around 1950. His mother and sister stand on the sidewalk before the flat and beam at the camera. Richards is ten feet away, decked out in a long coat and formal hat. His back is to the camera. His childhood for him is being too fat, too lonely, too ignorant to imagine the way out. He becomes a pacifist in high school, the notion a framework to control the anger boiling within him. In college, he thinks of being a writer but sidesteps to taste the camera. He plans on prison for refusing to fight in the war. He thinks, 'I'm against this war — I don't know about other wars. But this war is shit.' The boy stands with his back to the camera, the pacifist glowers with his hand unconsciously reaching for a gun, and inside both there is something to say and no real clear notion of how to say it.

And that leads him to a workshop with Minor White. The exercises entail shooting objects, photographic still lifes, and Richards recoils from this work but realizes it makes him see better. But White is more than technique for Richards, more than a belief in art as an absolute. He is a way to live. The simple home is white walls, very spare in look, green plants, select objects of beauty. White in memory is drinking, drinking hard, he is alive, and of course, the wood floors gleam with polish. The doors are open, not locked, the room glows with light, not Dorchester grey. Richards becomes a kind of factotum to White, the bright pupil helping out with workshops, the satellite to the new sun. But there is a crucial distance. 'He was a freak,' Richards tenderly recalls, using the word in a sixties sense of describing a man out of step with his times and by that act free of the shackles of his times. 'He knew I wasn't going to be an art photographer.' Minor White looks at Richards' photographs of gritty things from the streets and he says, 'You photograph people being eaten.' Richards is hurt, but some part of him understands what White is saying. This matter of mentorship, discipleship, this handing on of a tradition, is always messier in life than in the art histories. White transforms Richards and yet barely touches the core of his images. He gives him an attitude that photography matters, that looking matters. Richards becomes a thought: 'Never press the button unless it really matters.' All this happens so long ago, as Richards now sits on his sofa in the clean room with the soft light pouring through the windows. White died in 1975 and is now remembered in the history of photography as a man more important for what he believed than for the images he made. Richards is reaching back to the beginning of fifty-five photographs. 'I think,' he says, 'my feelings were what the hell was I going to do with the war? I felt that by focusing on damage, you were doing something quite positive. I thought it was something you had to do.' When he was a boy, he read the seminal American play of the nation reeling off World War II, *Death of a Salesman*. There is a line that rings in the head when every audience leaves a performance. Willy Loman, the salesman, has committed suicide. And his wife Linda says, 'Attention must be paid.' Richards stares at the white wall across the room from the sofa. His feet rest on polished wood floors in his Brooklyn home. The dog sleeps by the door downstairs, Janine works over accounts a floor below. He rifles the pile of plates and thinks back to Minor White, the wine, the plants, the open life, the dream of photography as art. Of the still lifes, the studio sensibility, he says, 'This is easier.' But everyone has to work out his own damnation. Gene Richards recalls almost wistfully, 'But I walked out there.'

She comes and goes. But is always here in the room. She is the first wife. Richards finds his way through the war by going to Arkansas and being a VISTA volunteer, an agency spawned by Lyndon Johnson's war on poverty as Johnson destroyed his political future with a war in Asia. Dorothea Lynch is also from Dorchester and one summer she goes south to visit his new strange life on the delta. It is the early seventies, the great civil rights bills are now law, the age of segregation is officially closed. But on the delta, on that pan of black dirt left by the floods of the Mississippi, that flat hot land spawning Elvis Presley, blues and hatred, the past is not yet over. Dorothea wants to be a writer and her talent is obvious. Richards wants to speak without lying and is not sure how. The initial work, VISTA, does not last long. Richards is booted out for what is seen as dissident ways. He and some other former VISTA workers found an organization, RESPECT, publish a paper and organize poor black people into some kind of entity that will make them more than they have been and what they have been are people kept down by whites. The hatred frightens Dorothea. She finds the gas jets turned on in their house, the lug nuts loosened on the tyres of their car.

He drives with two black women to a café and explains matter-of-factly, 'A guy tried to shoot us at a truckstop.' But that is not what really happens, not the part that matters. What really happens is 'I liked the people. I loved it there. I loved going up to the houses and not knocking on the door. I grew up in an Irish neighborhood and the doors were always locked. It made me feel alive.' He has found his place. The local coroner talks to him over the dead bodies, gives him the lives that have finally fled the flesh. He snaps a picture. Many pictures. But as he falls deeper in the black ground, he doubts what he is doing. There is something there and he thinks he is making pictures, not getting that something. 'I was always uncomfortable,' he remembers. 'It wasn't easy. You don't want to lie or hurt people with a camera. The people were complex. I take a picture of a blind woman but what I know is that she is fucking at night – she tells me this. I look at the picture and I can't see the fucking. The picture looks too simple. The people I see, the people in the pictures I take, the golden light of the delta doesn't fall on their faces. Visually, you start to fight against what had been exciting to you, because what had been exciting now becomes just a skill. And the skill kills content.' Rolling and tumbling, the delta nights caressing the skin, the smiles on black faces, the bleak-looking houses full of warm talk, the hunger to reach it and frame it and nail it and not lie. And the hatred of the whites for the other whites hanging out with the niggers. Richards finds a mangy, hairless and all but skinless dog tossed in a field to die. He nurses it back to health and calls the mutt Mange. The original owner finds out about this rescue and kills the dog. Richards snaps and buys a gun to kill the man who killed his dog. And then he comes back to himself and does not fire it. Dorothea typing, the hot night air coming through the window. The camera hectoring Richards, demanding he do something besides a cliché of injustice, black on white, the blues and segregation. The camera must take him past the document and into the flesh of the thing itself. There is a first picture that leads to all the others. He has burned rolls of film for years, but still there is this first picture. The group of men are black, the air chill, the ground bleak with winter. The casket is going into the ground for ever and one man looks over his shoulder smiling. Richards sits in Brooklyn feeling that day as he holds the print. Complexity, the jive ass messy nature of life, the scent coming off the women, the strong chords off the guitar in the bucket of blood saloons, click, right there for him in one frame. Now he thinks he can do it. For an instant he has seen the way. Maybe, he is a photographer. He leaves part of his mind in Arkansas. The whites find him out and beat him almost to death. He is evacuated to a Texas hospital. When he pulls out of it, his memory is crushed from the blows. He can go for about two weeks now, go and have a clear idea. Beyond that, it becomes a mist. The negatives are his memory. About ten years ago, Richards returned to the delta. He is driving down a road, crosses a concrete bridge and rolls up to a stop sign. A row of shacks comes into view. It looks familiar but he cannot be sure. Yes, it is in an old photo. Suddenly, a black woman comes out and leans into his window. She says, 'Hello, Gene. What took you so long to come back?' She goes into her shack and returns with a book wrapped in plastic. The thing was published in 1973 and is called *Few Comforts or Surprises: The Arkansas Delta*. Richards has returned to his pictures and they are his life. She slowly comes back to him out the mists.

He smiles as he recalls this, now safe in his house in Brooklyn. When I first met Richards we were working a story. Each night we'd return to our motel and I'd take him to his room. The beating, the frailty of memory. He was embarrassed at first over these random erasures that come and go in his memory. And then he relaxed and so each night I'd guide him to his room. It was not a large motel.

When he is finished with Arkansas, he and Dorothea return to Boston. He starts hanging out in Dorchester, now full of Puerto Ricans. He likes it, they are warm, they are like the delta. He makes *Dorchester Days* and he and Dorothea print it with their own little publishing venture. Then comes *50 Hours*, a span where he gets clubbed shooting a protest of a nuclear plant and in the same hours captures the birth of a child. He has found his way. Dorothea is a poet and she also writes words for the books. One morning she finds a lump on her breast. She writes the words, he takes the pictures. The book is called *Exploding Into Life*. She ends the book by dying. He shows the work to a curator. She says it is disgusting. He is devastated.

But Richards wins awards, gets grants. On paper, he is a success. He is the comer, the talent, the dark camera hunting the sunny land. He joins Magnum. He becomes part of *Life*. He is paid well. The evidence is in his lap as he sits in his fine house and flips through all those prints. He is seen as the heir to W. Eugene Smith, he is seen as the next Robert Frank. The shambling man, the fat child who turns away, the camera that can barely be seen since Richards becomes invisible after a few moments. His delicate hands move carefully through the fifty-five plates. He becomes a stream of fragmentary sentences. The brick through his car window, the black man in Boston who drags him off and saves his life. Chicago is that twelve-year-old in the project who is pregnant. The beautiful woman in the insane asylum crammed into a locker with a man and fucking. A friend touches the hair of his mentally ill son. Gene gives him the picture and the friend says, 'That is not a nice picture. But it is true.' A face in the frame, and Richards says, 'She disappeared that night, she's probably dead.' A woman in a kitchen and he says, 'This is the story that got me fired.' He says, 'Take this check and shove it up your ass.' Richards is back there, for seconds, for moments, back there fifty-five times. The man who has trouble remembering because of the beating cannot seem to ever really forget the real stuff. And the real stuff is a wound, a wound that cannot heal, one caused by some event that cannot be said or maybe recalled, but the wound seeps, never really scars over, and he can touch the wound and then he is back, the dates scrambled, the fat woman coming out of the house with the old photo book wrapped in plastic, her name floating just out of Richards' grasp, but he is back, it is all really in his head, none of it is lost, it just lacks names and dates and sometimes geography, but it is anchored and it is anchored by this wound. Somehow the man who cannot find his motel room manages to wander the backwaters of Africa, Central America and North America and always find the shot.

The room in Brooklyn is Minor White but the man in the room is Eugene Richards. He looks ahead, his eyes slightly downcast but still ahead, and he says of Dorothea, 'She just filled up a room. She was actually very shy. The cancer gave her a chance to come out.' The second marriage is good. The boy is the apple of Richards' eye. Janine comes up the stairs with more coffee. She is the floor Richards stands on, the roof that shelters him, the person who understands in a world where he feels alone. This must be what the dream felt like when Minor White opened the door and the room exploded with space light, beautiful things, talk, gleaming floors. Books would be on the shelf, prints on the wall, purpose in the heart. Lots of wine and maybe some roses.

The price is never mentioned and even later it is hard to describe. Once you know, you have to live with the knowing. Once you feel, you must put the feeling into the thing at hand. And doing this costs. But you become addicted to the price. You fight it. You keep raising the stakes, making the photos offhanded almost smeared and out of kilter, fighting pretty pictures, fighting easy pictures, lusting after success and resenting success when it comes because you cannot trust success, it feels like betrayal, betrayal of what you see and feel, betrayal of the people who let you slip into their lives, you, a fat child turning his back to the camera, and the pictures fill you with pride and yet fill you with a kind of self-hatred, pride in what you see, disappointment in what you did not get, that thing on your tongue, that thing floating all around you as you work, that trust people give you, that bounce in the step, that swing in the hip, there are songs, goddammit, real songs going on while you work, and all you have is a still photograph, fifty-five of the goddamn things, your life, shit you are middle-aged, they are piled on your lap. And still you feel empty. She is always in the room.

He wishes he could write and in fact he writes well. But he feels he can't quite get it on paper, maybe the beatings ruined that part for him. He sometimes wonders about that.

I'm sitting on the sofa, Gene Richards is sitting beside me talking but he does not turn to me, he looks straight ahead, he is doing that middle-distance talk the stuff soldiers slip into when they, very rarely, are willing to return to the war, to the actual moment, and when they do that, they slip unconsciously into the present tense because the war then is not past, it is here, right here in the safe room. We are almost there, to the point we have been heading. He has ticked off his photographs, his lifetime reduced to one shot a year. And I like the photographs, think they nail what I have seen but cannot say. I am the fan, the safe listener. I've researched the dull bones of the life, the Minor White stuff, the delta, Dorothea exploding into life, the awards, the battles with *Life* magazine, the years with Magnum, the days on the streets feeding the camera crack and the night the cops insisted he wear a flak jacket for *Cocaine True, Cocaine Blue*, the Guggenheim award, the prizes, the exhibitions, the becoming a kind of adjective in the business, a Gene Richards shot or story, the thing the kids coming up want to be. Trolled through the changes in the business, the death of the mainstream magazines that featured photo-essays, the war by the colour slicks against black-and-white images, the long jaunts to hellholes in Africa and Latin America looking for all the deltas and Dorchesters the world needs to face.

He's kept the faith, one that he cannot quite say but one he feels, and that faith is to get the world down with a camera, to tell stories with pictures, to paint scenes magazines do not want, to insist on a still photograph in a world of television, film and video streaming through cyberspace. Lately, he's been taking a stab at film with some short documentaries and he still has this desire to write. To keep his home rolling he does some advertising shoots. His life, with some adjusting here and there, can be made to look normal, striving and within acceptable boundaries. But it is not acceptable. It is a calling, though he would wince at the word and start sputtering denials. And the call is coming from the people inside the photographs.

We are getting closer, I can feel it, getting closer to the silence of photographs
the infuriating silence that fills Gene Richards' pacifist heart with rage. He
says, 'Photography has never been easy for me, it's always been painful. Picking
up that camera has always been hard for me … If someone says "no" to me, i
means "no" and I go away … I could sense in all this beauty there was something not quite right.' I remember when we were working a story in a rich Texas
town where the rich children of the rich parents were busy dying from heroin
overdoses. The town was big houses, dead malls full of merchandise, blan
white faces behind the wheels of fancy cars. Gene wandered with me for a da
down the empty cold streets and finally said, 'There is nothing here to
photograph.' I said, 'That's why I want you to make it a picture.'

Now, in the grey light of Brooklyn, he stares down at one picture and says, '
took it nervously. I was going crazy. The terrible silence. I took it for reasons .
don't even know. Taking these kinds of pictures – throughout my whole lifetime in
photography I've always known that what I do is an isolated and rare artefact
The people I come from wouldn't understand. As art, there is a lot of confusion
about what the fuck pictures are. I used to think I was creating excitement. Now
I think they are a piece of history. Now I want to see the truth of the pictures.
consider my career as a photographer to be pretty much over. I'm fifty-five
This book is chronological. I've never done this before. I didn't grow, I'm the
same photographer as when I was twenty-five. This is strange. The pictures are
becoming increasingly silent. There is an assumption that pictures speak. They
don't. The silence of the pictures is starting to bother me. I'm failing, failing to
provide the context that it is important that you know.' And then he falls silent in
the face of the silence of photographs. We both stare at an old breast hanging
off a black woman. A child rests on her back. The picture is cropped, we canno

see her face, nor her hips, nor her legs. She is in Africa. The child is her grandchild and she is walking for ever to reach a clinic to save the child. She does not know the child is dying. She does not know she will become a huge cropped image, the skin rich and black and so inviting I want to caress it. I want to rub my face against this photograph. My eyes open and eat the image.

I tell him that he can't quit doing this because this is what he does. He sighs and begins talking about this terrible silence, about his conversation with the woman, about the context, the smells and love and laughter and death surrounding the beautiful black skin in the print. About what he has to get down, capture, and how he has failed. It is not enough, never enough. So much out there. A fat child turns from the camera. Then turns back.

His feet are now on the polished wood floor, he looks away from me at the clean white wall in the grey light.
'You have to know more about her,' he says.
'Yes, but now I finally know she exists and feel her sweeping through my flesh. And the old woman has finally touched my life.

He's talking, talking fifty-five times and it is all one photograph. And all one long sentence.

A Soldier's Home, Hughes, Arkansas, 1970. He stands tall in that photograph but when you find him twenty years later he is embittered because his life has not worked out and because you no longer remember him and how do you talk about the beatings life has given both of you? and besides, he fit into the frame before you knew what you were doing but he became part of the way to the next thirty years of your life

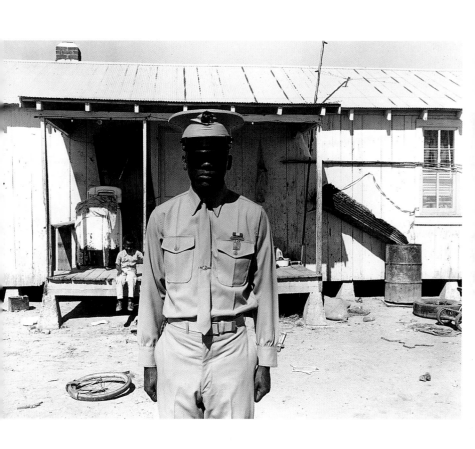

Logan's Mortuary, West Memphis, Arkansas, 1971. and Jesus, he'd talk, and the body is on the table and all these things you could not see and the camera did not know, all that stuff would come tumbling out as the cold steel instruments pressed against the now still flesh

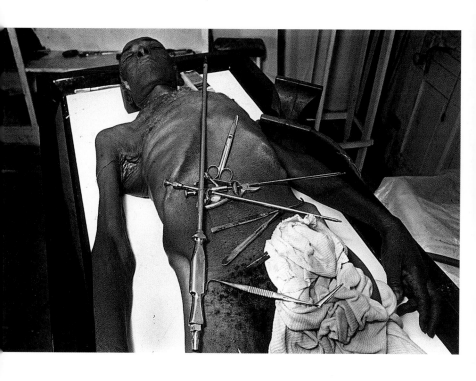

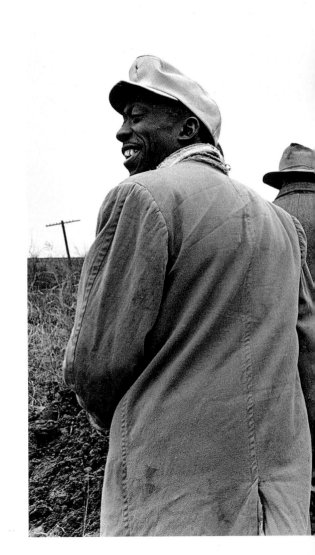

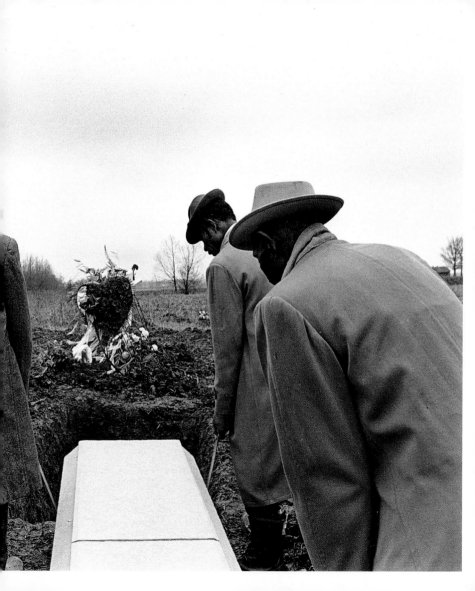

(previous page) Funeral for Eddie Collins, Forrest City, Arkansas, 1971. and they're getting maybe fifty cents for carrying the stiff, the trees stand bare, the hats and coats look solid and down and then the guy turns, flashes that smile, and you suddenly believe in your work because you have seen life and caught life at the burying ground

Puerto Rican Bride, Dorchester, Massachusetts, 1974. and they are alive, the women hot, the buildings weigh a ton, and you want it just right, drifting off the bottom of the frame like an afterthought, because it is too important

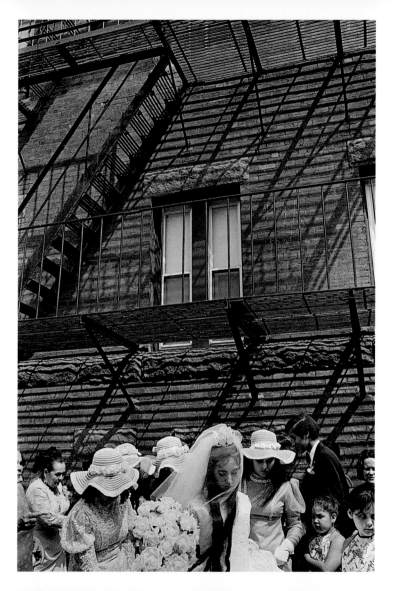

Family Argument, Dorchester, Massachusetts, 1975. and what is important is the warmth inside the cold walls where you once grew up and what is important is the chicken, so much depends on a chicken within the walls of Dorchester, Massachusetts

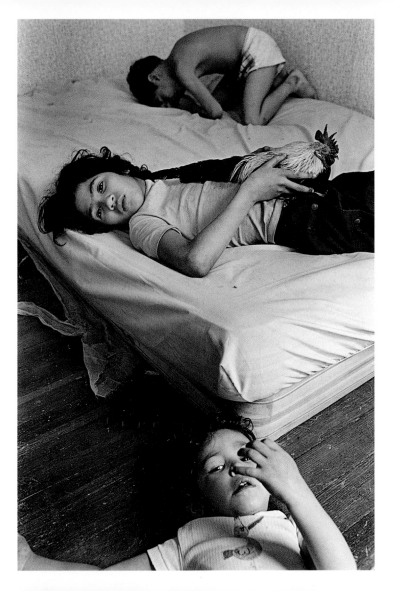

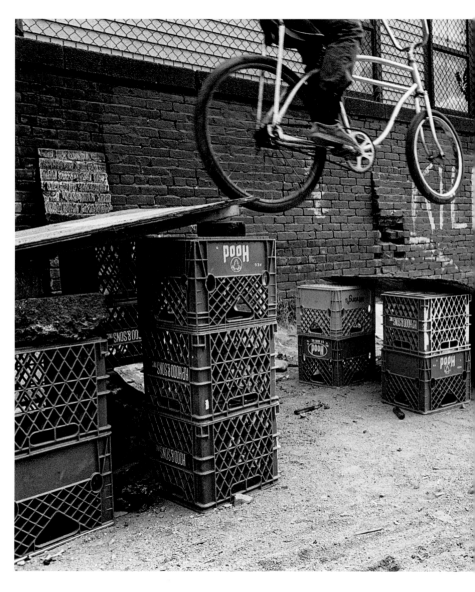

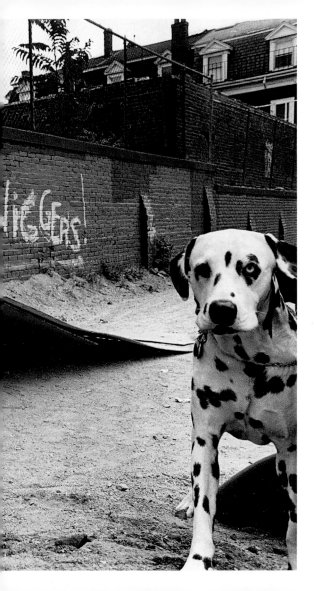

(previous page) Graffiti, South Boston, 1975. but there is this thing outside the lens, this thing shimmering and ready to erupt, this thing off the pages of the newspapers but in the streets, something about race and hatred and the damn kid is on his bike, God, the arc of his move, you wish you could have done that and then this missing thing is there

Dorothea, Boston, Massachusetts, 1979. Dorothea wants to get it all down, going to make a book out of this, and the doctor enters, looks at you like you're some kind of bug to be taking pictures at such a moment and then he turns to Dorothea and says, 'Does it make you feel like less of a woman?' and she laughs, you're clicking away as she laughs and you don't know until later that you've got it and then you don't know what you've got

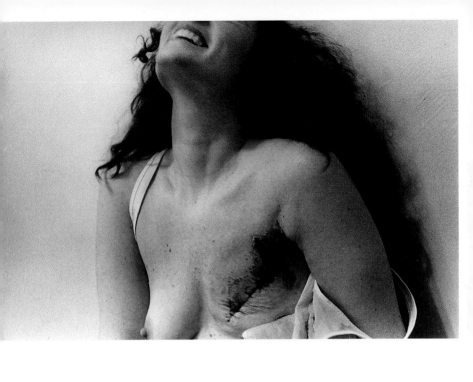

Birth of Henry Harry, Jamaica Plain, Massachusetts, 1979. and you see birth for the first time during this fifty hours of turbulence and you are not ready but you are hungry

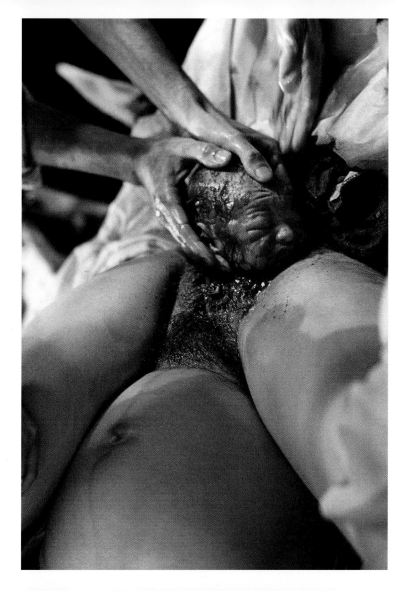

Hospital for the Criminally Insane, Lima, Ohio, 1981. and he is in the crazy place in Lima, Ohio, drinking gallons of soft drinks every day until his face disintegrates and after a while you just move in there and live there and keep shooting

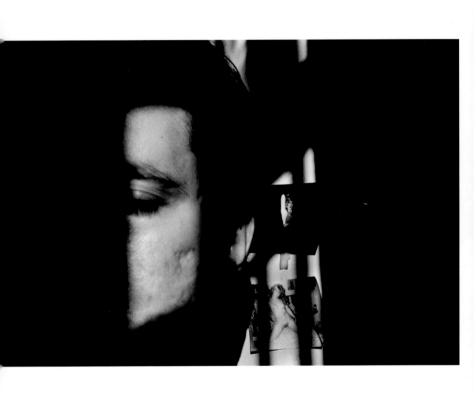

Exhausted Nurse, Denver, Colorado, 1982. and the appetite rises and you become addicted to the emergency room where life fits your feelings

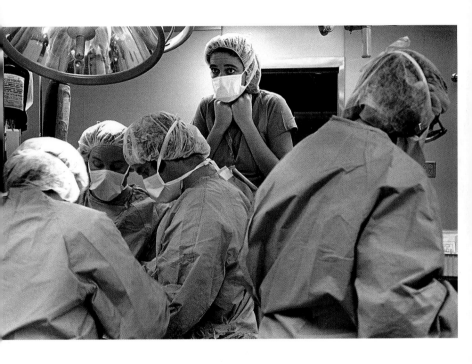

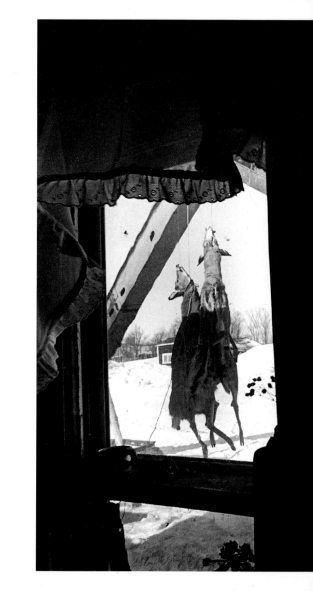

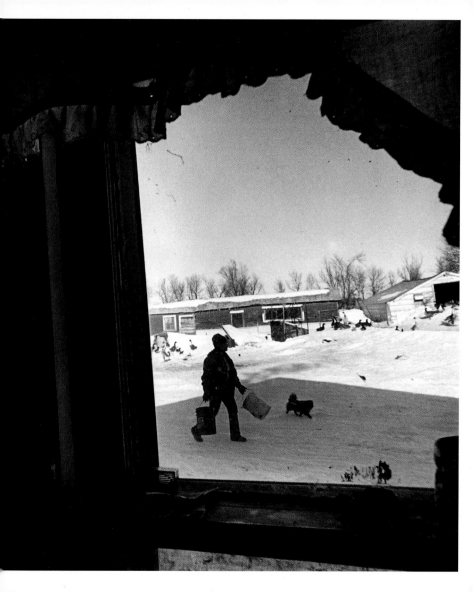

(previous page) **Farm Facing Foreclosure, Gann Valley, South Dakota, 1985.** and it was supposed to be safe here but it is not and then you look up and you know how to do something and you make a picture

Return from Prison, New York City, 1986. and the crack is the air, he's just gotten out of the joint, you snap the picture and that night she disappears for ever

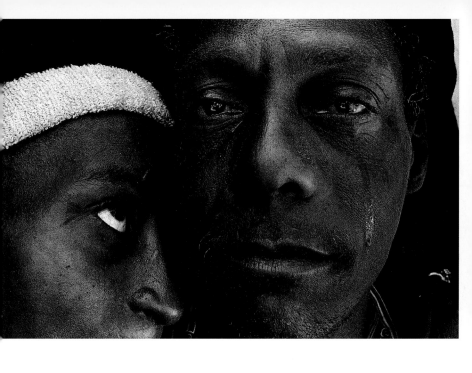

Henry's Boots, Still House Hollow, Tennessee, 1986. and he is crazy about the boots, polishing them every day, no money, just dreams, but the boots

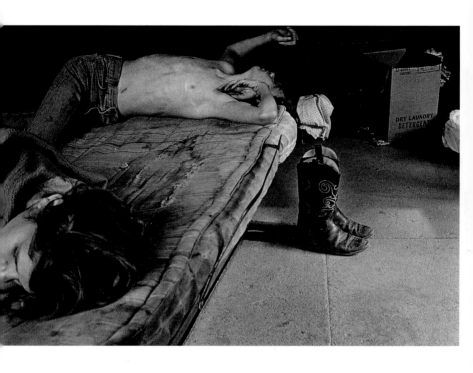

Village Elder with River Blindness, Guinea, 1988. and he'd been a head man when the river blindness came and now he stares through eyes gone dark as the light pours through the tear in the wall

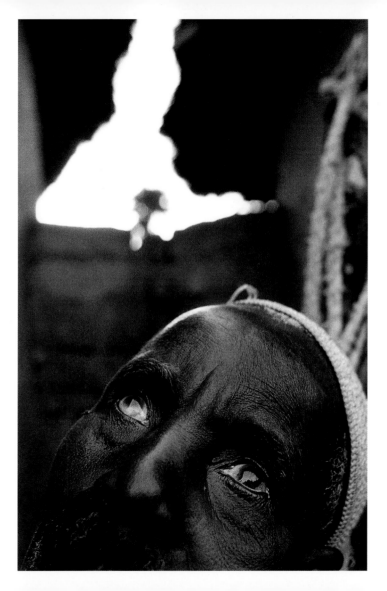

Village, Guinea, 1988. and the leg looks too thin, the chicken too anxious but the huts seem warm

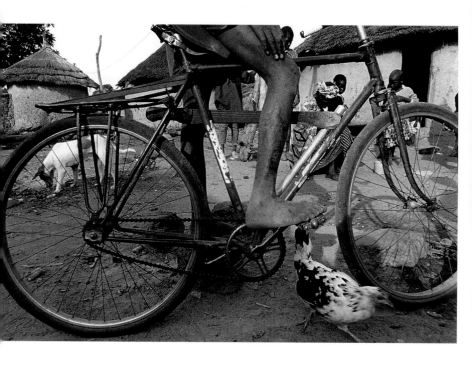

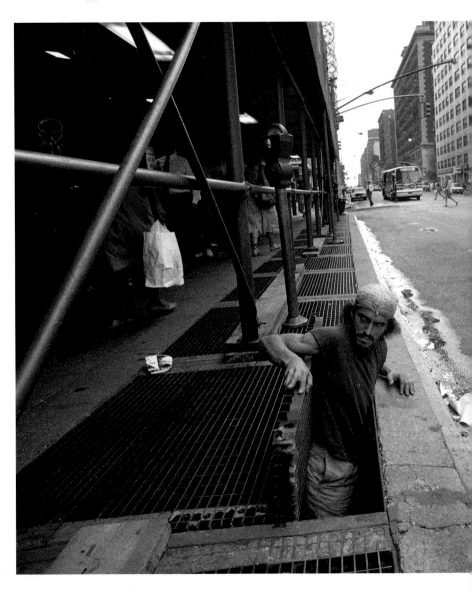

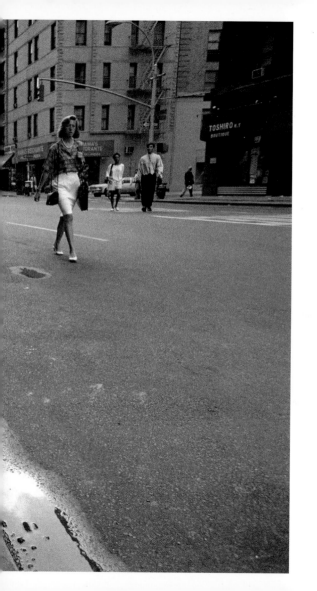

(previous page) Tom, New York City, 1988. and he comes at people, the weak and the helpless, with a knife and he takes and now he is emerging for the hunt in the richest city of the world and she is walking down the avenue as if none of this exists, so safe in her fine shoes

Pop Myles' Gym, East St Louis, Illinois, 1989. and the room is so cold but the town fathers know the big camera is coming and so they get some heat so it will look good

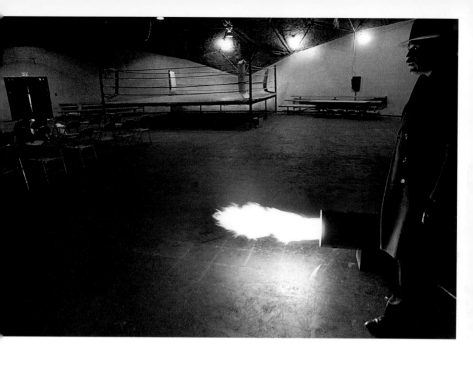

'Ruthless', North Philadelphia, Pennsylvania, 1990. and he wants the world to see the guns of crack and you say, 'You know the cops will hunt you?' and he turns and fires one into a building

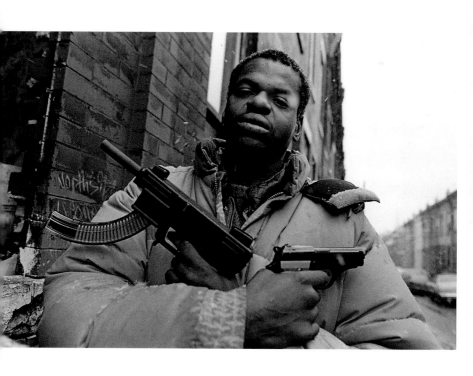

Crack House, North Philadelphia, Pennsylvania, 1990. and she wants crack and that is all that matters and they don't care that you are there but still they fee your presence and he can never quite get it up

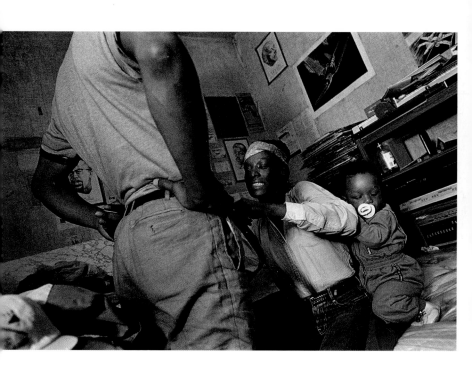

Arrest, North Philadelphia, Pennsylvania, 1990. and with a snap of the hand-cuffs some local guys suddenly become them, the suspects removed from the street, and the street, of course, goes on with its life as if they had never existed

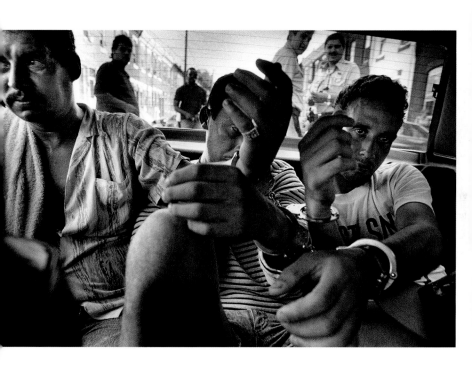

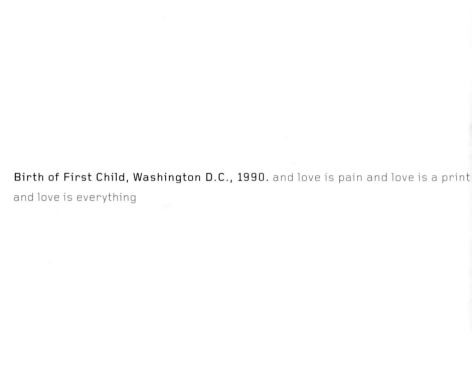

Birth of First Child, Washington D.C., 1990. and love is pain and love is a print and love is everything

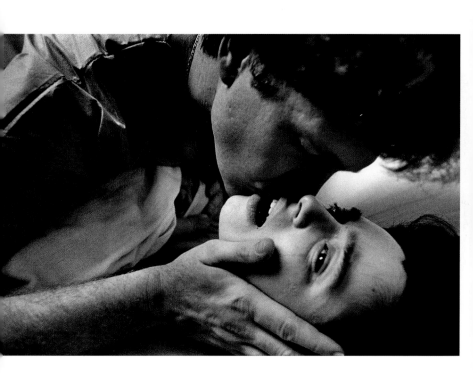

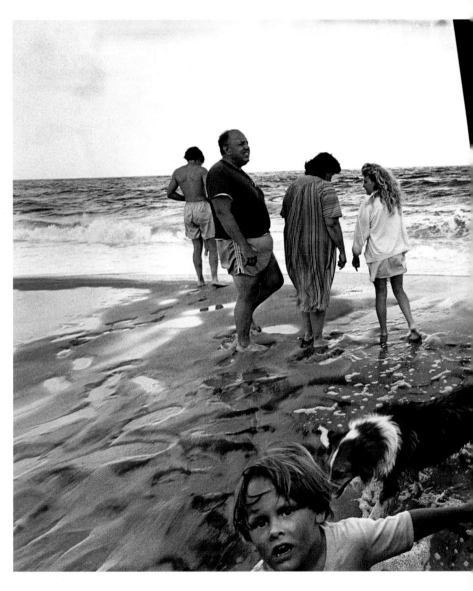

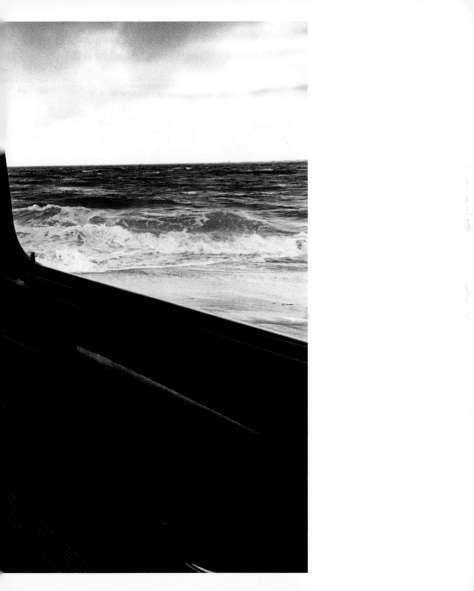

(previous page) **Father of Twelve, Cape Hatteras, North Carolina, 1990.** and you have to know the long tired air of the house in the city to feel the rush when the car door opens

Morning, Isleta, New Mexico, 1990. and, God, her man had been in a gang but now he's on the straight path and that is why so much depends on the kids in the sink and facing morning with sun in the window

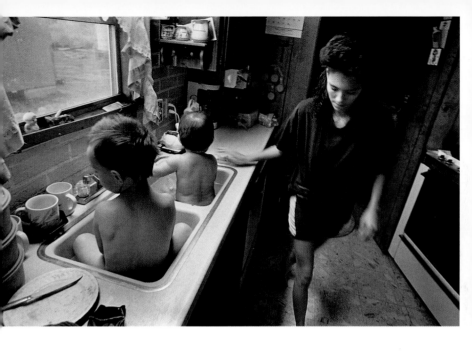

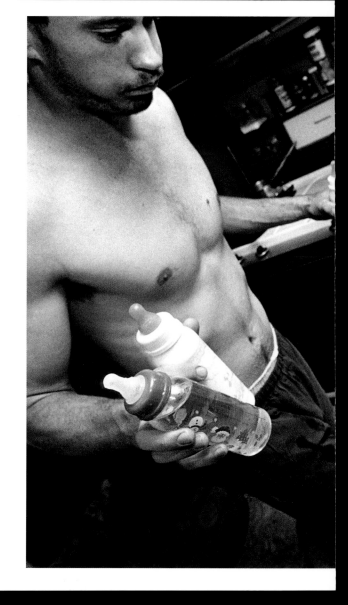

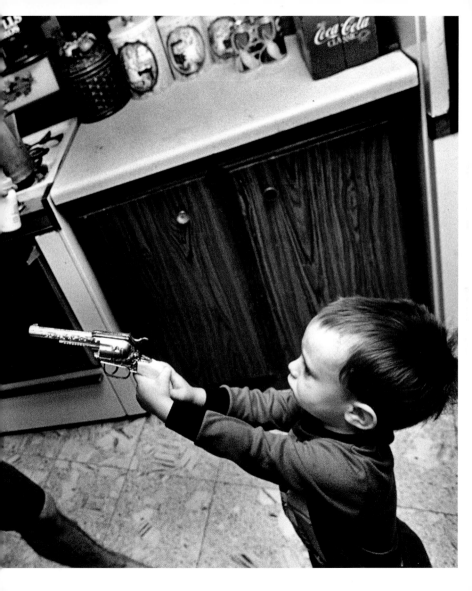

(previous page) Father and Son, Isleta, New Mexico, 1990. and so you fight to get right with the world and be a parent and a wage earner and something people treat with respect, something no longer called a problem

Classroom, Uganda, 1991. and you just take the picture because it means people are trying and then you hang around and learn nothing is happening here, everything is crumbling

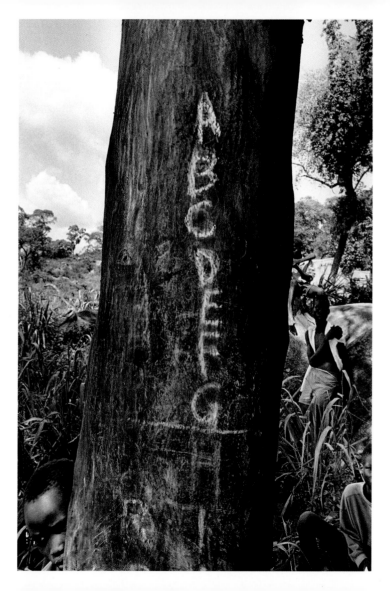

Afraid for His Sick Wife, Uganda, 1991. and he has come to feed her in the hospital and each time he puts a spoon of food in her mouth, she takes it out and puts it in his mouth, so don't tell me about love

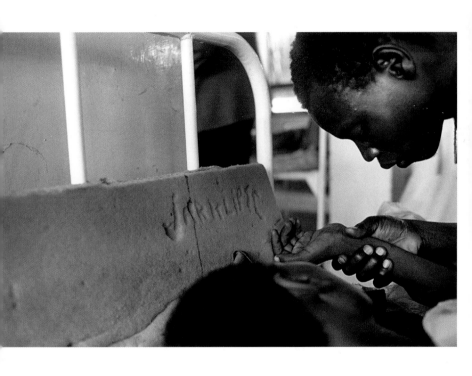

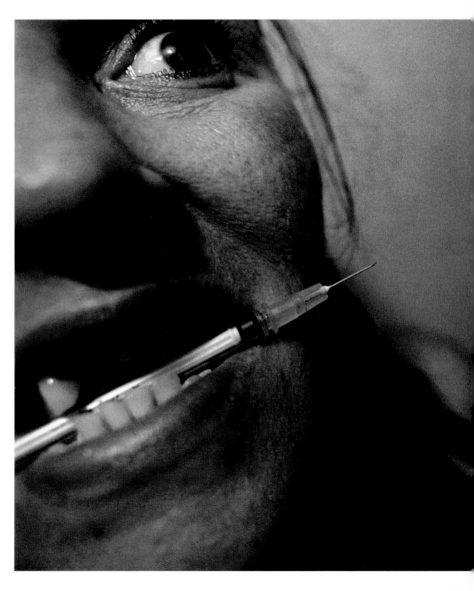

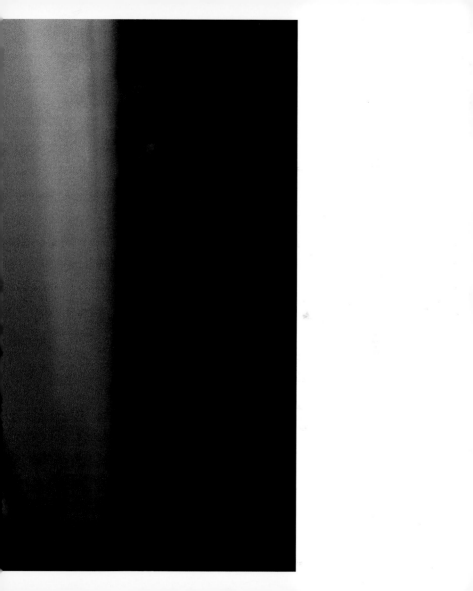

(previous page) **Mariella, East New York, 1992.** and the needle says everything you can't find words for

The Son He Abandoned, East New York, 1992. and you can love hard and love deep and still fail and the authorities take your son away from you and now let's fix it

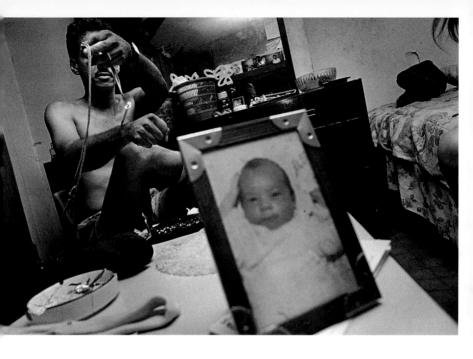

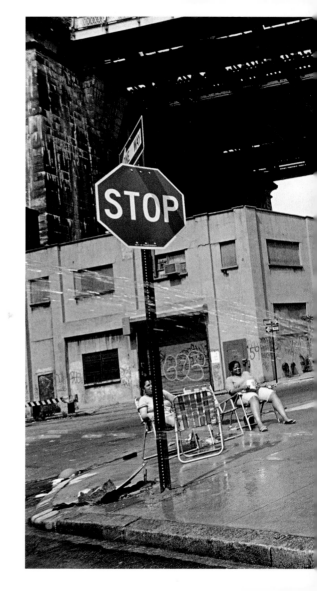

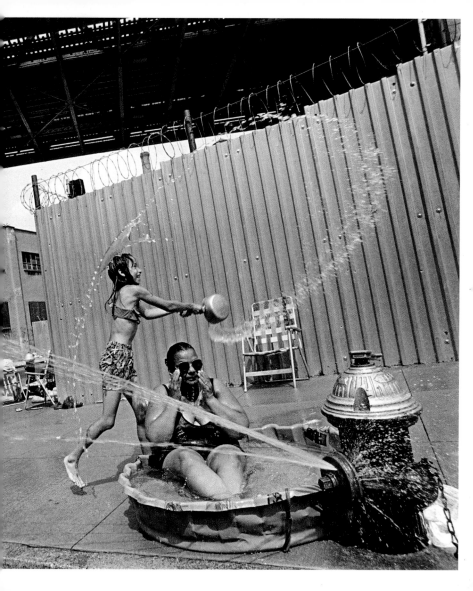

(previous page) Grandmother, Brooklyn, New York, 1993. and you come out of the subway and suddenly see this and your soul smiles and you make a picture and then after talking you know a daughter is watching from down the street and she cannot be in this frame because she's got problems and you begin to dread the silence of photographs

Serbian Military Hospital, Bosnia, 1993. and you get the shot of the endless pain in the heart of Europe returning once again to that dark night, but the magazine does not want the image because it is of a Serb suffering and they are at that moment not popular and so their pain is of no account

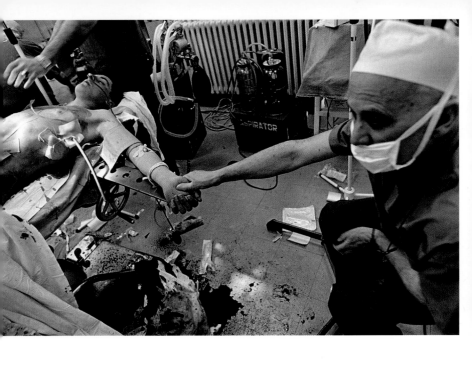

Gay Parents, Washington D.C., 1993. well, hell, some of them donated sperm and being the biological dad isn't what's important here because they love the boy and take care of him and so who's to say? who's to mess up a family with judgements no one wants?

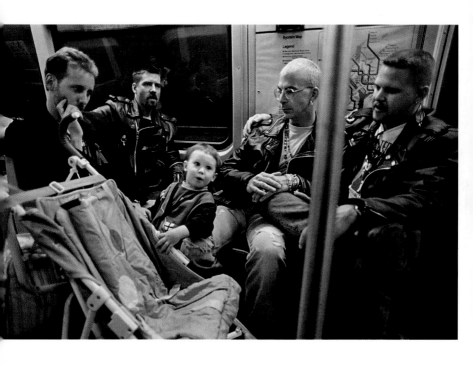

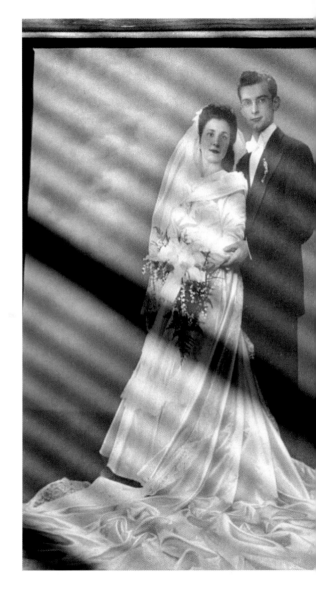

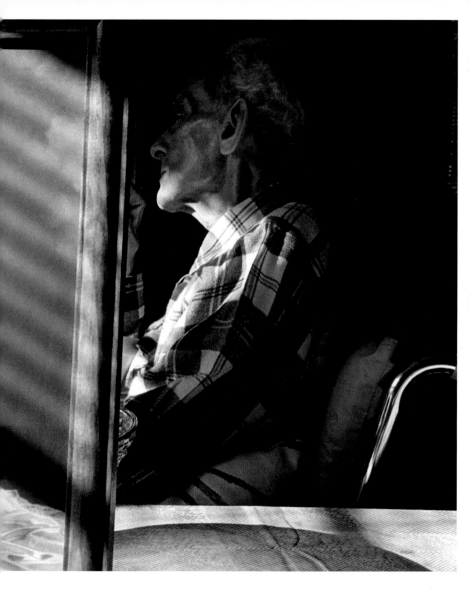

(previous page) Andrew, Staten Island, 1994. and you know the distance between the old photo and the one you are making is the distance of a lifetime the private journey from the flame to the ashes as the room closes in on every thing but memory

Murder Scene, Bronx, New York, 1994. and he opened the door, bang! just like that and nothing more to say

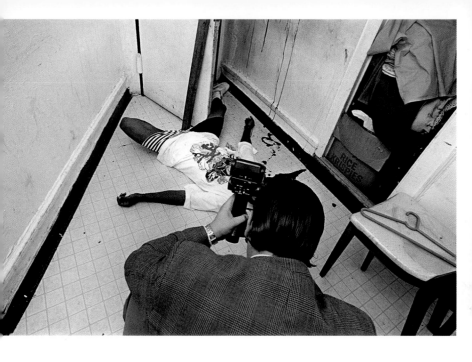

Children of the Blind, Niamey, Niger, 1994. and it looks so lovely but the shadows are kids used as seeing-eye dogs for the blind and the locals say, hey, we only pick the ugly dumb kids for the work, but one of these kids spends his spare time hanging out in a hotel lobby and watching CNN and he picks up four or five languages this way and people notice and now that one kid is in London going to school

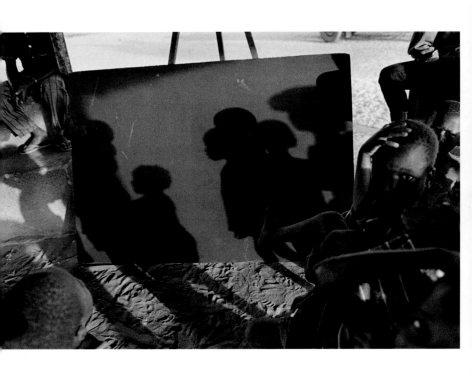

Morning, Brooklyn, New York, 1994. and to be your wife on clean sheets meeting dawn in the sun of your boy's boundless energy

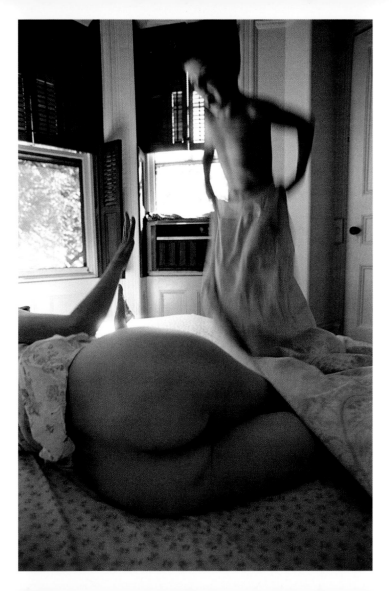

Sam and Our Dog Tom, Brooklyn, New York, 1994. and you want the world to be
your son in his house in his bathtub with his dog

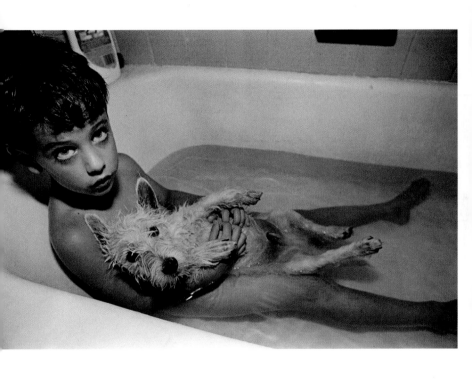

Robert Frank and His Son Pablo, New York City, 1994. and even memory can sear as the father gently caresses the hair of his son who will in time die young

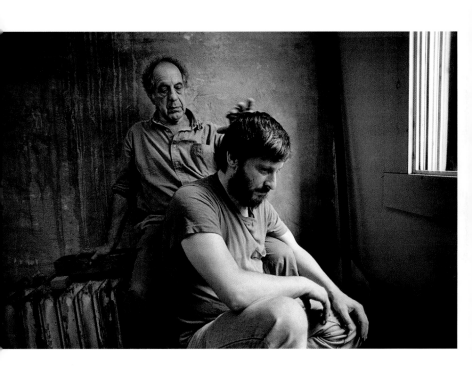

Street Gang, Kansas City, Missouri, 1995. and yet you know she's officially a teenager and everyone is stoned and suddenly everyone goes over the edge and it's right there, about to happen, the cards are up in the air and you don't know what's going down or what you are going to do and her boyfriend is sitting there rubbing his nose like nothing is happening and then, fuck, somehow everyone lets out their breath and it doesn't happen

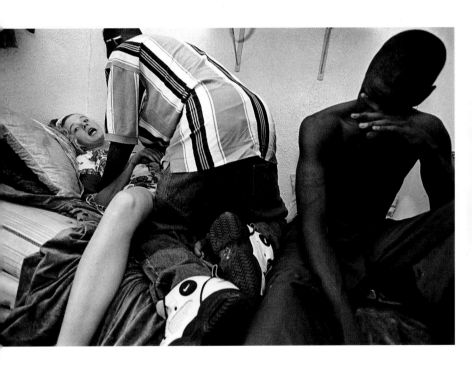

Rex and Inez Colerick, Auburn, Nebraska, 1995. and they are getting old an you can feel death on their shoulders and no image is enough for what you see

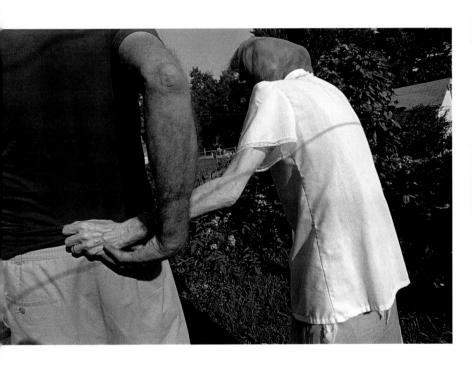

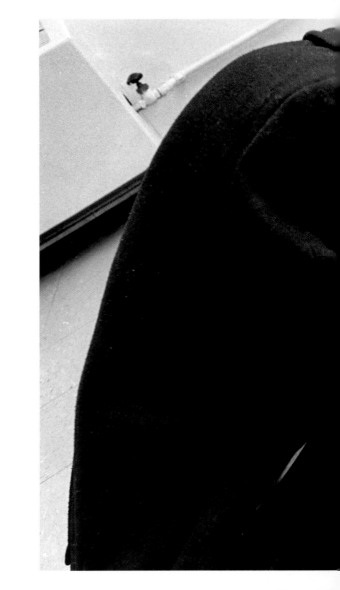

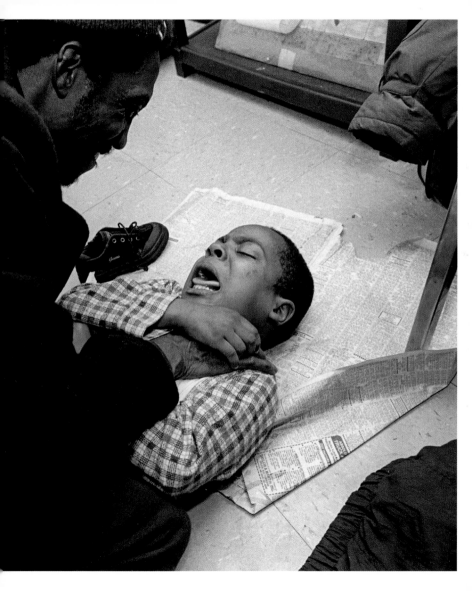

(previous page) Abuse, Chicago, Illinois, 1995. and love can be hard and love can be wrong and there are places where the parents savage the children and do not recognize this fact and you take the photo because others must know what you now know

Mourning the Death of a Fellow Cop, Philadelphia, Pennsylvania, 1996. and the morning fills with death, no matter how much polish is given the leather, the brass, still the early morning sags with death and the fact that it is the death of a brother officer means you are still alive and means you could die just like that and other cops will get up early and get the polish

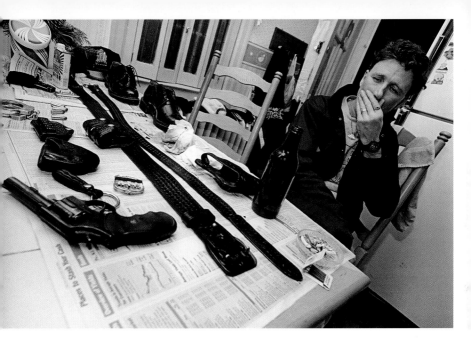

The Grave of a Slave, Farmville, Virginia, 1996. and maybe you think the best cure is forgetting and then you stumble on the old grave in the woods poking like a sharp tooth through the fallen leaves and then you know once again that the past can be forgotten for a while but refuses to go away

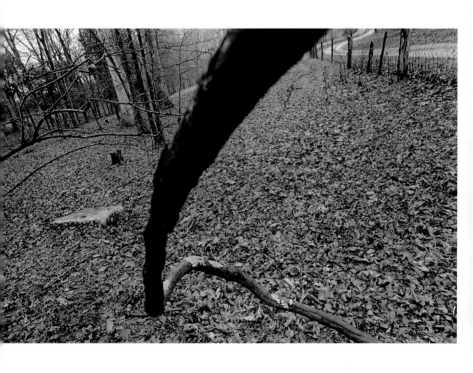

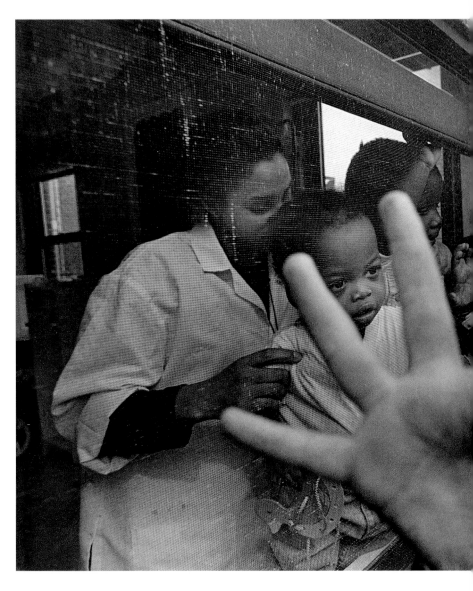

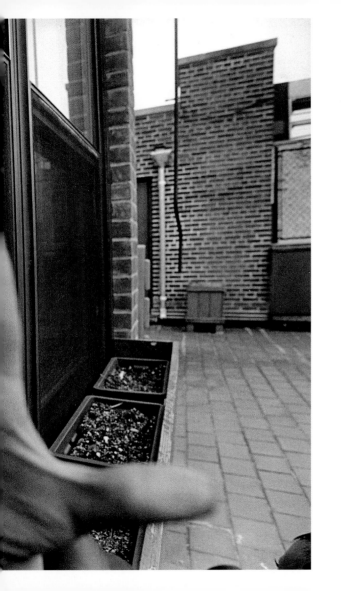

(previous page) Incarnation Children's Center, Washington Heights, New York, 1997. and most of the kids are HIV positive but they don't all know it and they'll live because of medicines but no one knows what such a life means and the hand reaches in front of the camera and says pay attention to me

Death from AIDS, Washington Heights, New York, 1997. and he wasn't very old and he wasn't very big and you don't know what else to say with your camera

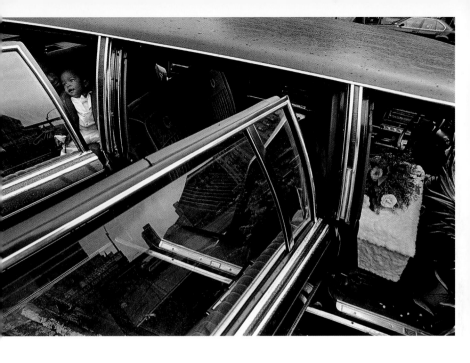

Competition for Momma's Breast, Honduras, 1997. because it flows through us like milk, it keeps coming, no matter how bleak the shack, how thin the meals, the breast round and full of milk, your mouth, you can always feel your mouth on that breast no matter what happens later

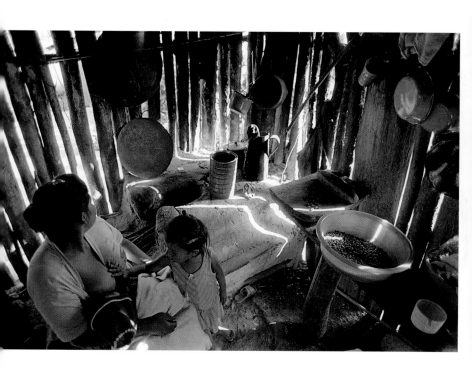

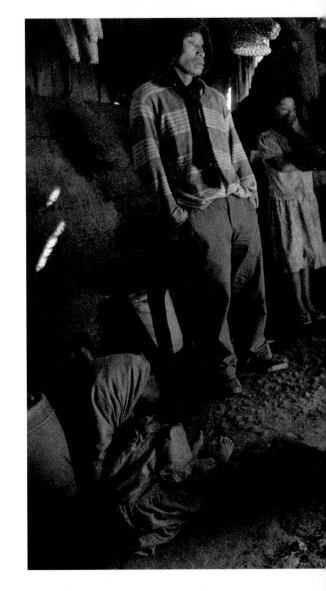

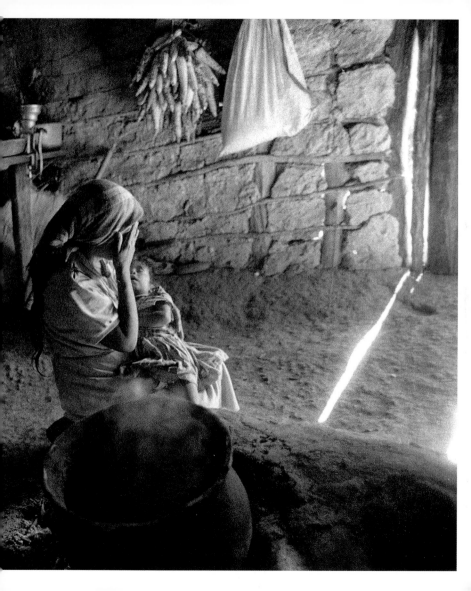

(previous page) Suffering Pneumonia, Honduras, 1997. no matter how much cold, no matter how many children die, no matter how helpless everyone becomes as the death rattle snakes up an infant's throat

The Road to Safo, Niger, 1997. and they eat the earth itself and still there is not enough for all the mouths

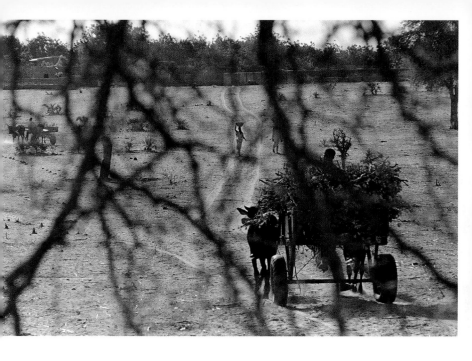

Malnutrition, Safo, Niger, 1997. and she is eighty-one, walking miles to save her grandchild and you ask can you take the picture what with her breasts hanging down and she says you think I care at my age and you snap it and the child dies later and the old woman says hey there are old people in America and you should take me home and I'll take care of your old people because no one needs me here

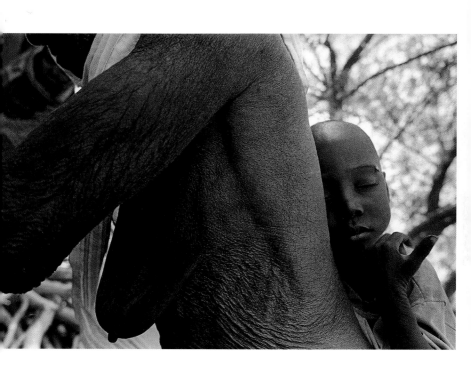

Toy, Safo, Niger, 1997. you can't walk past the toy because even here, yes, here, play still exists as a part of the dream

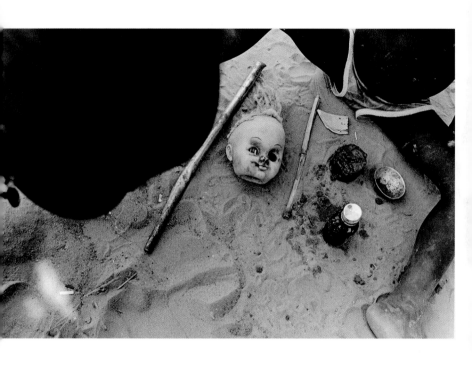

Infant Suffering AIDS, Safo, Niger, 1997. and her husband is a trucker an

she's just a kid and AIDS owns her but she doesn't notice and you feed off th

sweat glistening on her fine face and

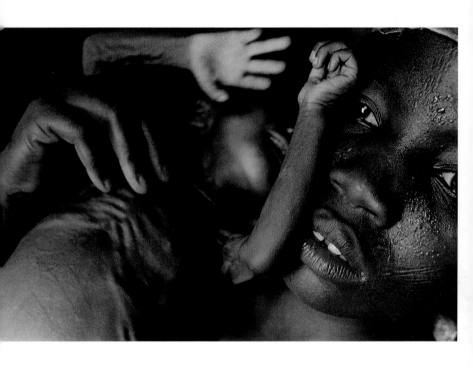

A Catch of Crawdaddies, Greeley, Colorado, 1999. you're doing a story or working in the slaughterhouses, and the guy you are tracking has had his body broken by the work and you get depressed and you go out and see the crawdaddies kids have gathered to sell for bait and it is so refreshing and God suddenly you feel your head clear and you snap the picture for yourself and to hell with the world, you need this floor of crawdaddies in a red wagon if you are to stand but then the kids start tossing the crawdaddies around as if they're just things and you are back where you started and

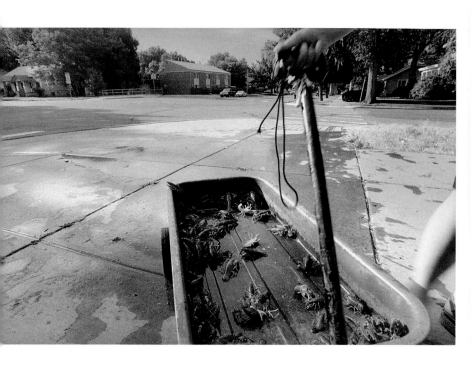

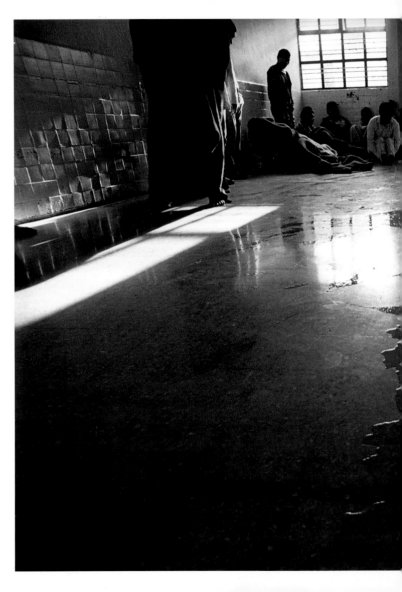

(previous page) Men's Ward, Psychiatric Hospital, Mexico, 1999. you love this shot, love the form of the puddle of urine, the light falling through the windows the people haunting the background and you want to scream because it is a pretty picture that does not say these people are insane and that some are not insane, are just people society dumped and warehoused and now they're living in filth and unloved and fuck the light and the puddle and

Abandoned, Psychiatric Hospital, Mexico, 1999. she started out sucking her thumb and then went for it and that is her fist in her mouth and she is seventeen and living in the crazy place and this is the shot but they don't like it because it is too close and people say you are difficult and you think just look at her and this should go in the magazine because

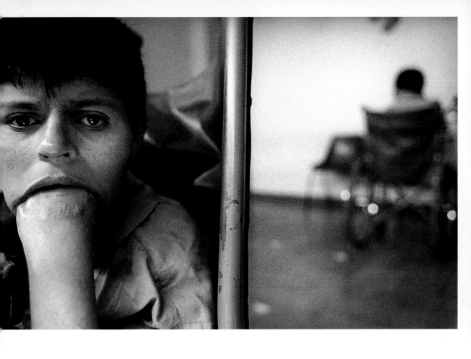

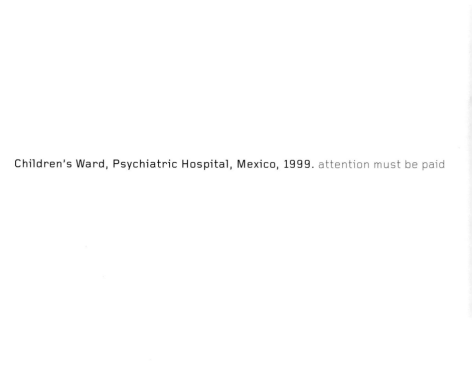

Children's Ward, Psychiatric Hospital, Mexico, 1999. attention must be paid

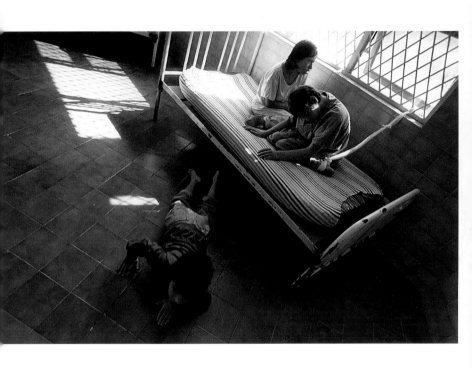

My Mother at the End of Her Life, Port Orange, Florida, 1999. because that is your mother dying and that is your 91-year-old father denying that she is dying and you take this picture and it is a metaphor for death and it is a metaphor for love and it is an invasion of privacy and it is too goddamn silent because that is not a metaphor that is your mother on an exact day in an exact place and she is dying before your eyes.

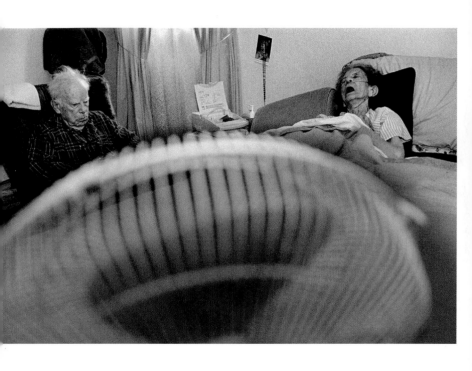

1944 Born 25 April, Dorchester, Massachusetts. Father is a shipyard painter, mother works as a house cleaner.

1963–1967 Attends Northeastern University. Meets Dorothea Lynch, his first wife. Active against the war in Vietnam.

1967–1968 Completes degree in English and Journalism. Studies photography at MIT with Minor White.

1969–1972 Joins VISTA and works as a health worker in the Mississippi River delta, Arkansas. Helps found RESPECT, which distributes food and clothing to the poor. Photographs the lives of the area's people.

1973 Returns to Dorchester. Publishes first book, *Few Comforts or Surprises: The Arkansas Delta*. Receives a National Endowment for the Arts grant.

1974 Begins work as a freelance editorial photographer.

1978 Self-publishes his second book, *Dorchester Days*. Becomes nominee member of Magnum. Begins documentary of Dorothea Lynch's ordeal with breast cancer.

1979–1980 Photographs Denver General's emergency room, and nuclear testing in islands in South Pacific.

1980 Receives Guggenheim Fellowship.

1981 Receives W. Eugene Smith Memorial Award. Made full member of Magnum. Moves to New York. Covers wars in Beirut and El Salvador.

1983 Death of Dorothea. Self-publishes *50 Hours*.

1986 Publishes *Exploding Into Life*, photographs and diary of Dorothea's struggle with cancer. Wins the Book of the Year Award.

1987 Is named Photojournalist of the Year by ICP, New York, for documentation of poverty, 'Below the Line: Living in Poor America'. With Janine Altongy, has a son, Sam.

1988 Begins work on illegal drugs in America.

1989 Publishes *The Knife and Gun Club: Scenes from an Emergency Room*.

1990 Begins series on the American family for *Life* magazine and photographs health conditions in Uganda. Is named POY Magazine Photographer of the Year.

1992–1993 Photographs English farming, river blindness in Africa, the Wetlands in Nigeria, which wins Leica Oskar Barnack Award. Directs short video documentary *Cocaine True, Cocaine Blue*.

1994–1995 Publishes *Cocaine True, Cocaine Blue* (Kraszna-Krausz Award), and *Americans We* (ICP Infinity Book Award). Photographs pediatric heart surgery in Guatemala, ageing and death in America, homicide detectives. Resigns from Magnum.

1996 Completes series for *Life* on American communities. Is named POY Magazine Photographer of the Year.

1997 Documents health conditions in a Niger village, impoverished Honduran campesinos, a Kansas City street gang, the life of a Philadelphia police officer, and American children with HIV and AIDS.

1998 Receives the Robert F. Kennedy Lifetime Achievement Journalism Award and is named POY Magazine Photographer of the Year.

1999 Produces a film, *Arruyo Mi Niño: I Hug My Child*. Documents residents in mental institutions in Mexico.

2000 Completes the film *but, the day came*, which is awarded Jury Prize for Best Short Film at DoubleTake Documentary Film Festival.

Photography is the visual medium of the modern world. As a means of recording, and as an art form in its own right, it pervades our lives and shapes our perceptions.

55 is a new series of beautifully produced, pocket-sized books that acknowledge and celebrate all styles and all aspects of photography.

Just as Penguin books found a new market for fiction in the 1930s, so, at the start of a new century, Phaidon **55**s, accessible to everyone, will reach a new, visually aware contemporary audience. Each volume of 128 pages focuses on the life's work of an individual master and contains an informative introduction and 55 key works accompanied by extended captions.

As part of an ongoing program, each **55** offers a story of modern life.

Eugene Richards (b.1942) has created a body of work that is considered one of the most outstanding and significant of contemporary photojournalism. His images unflinchingly confront the less than pleasant truths of modern life and are testimony to his commitment to social justice. Recently he has turned to documentary film-making, again highlighting social issues.

Charles Bowden has been a reporter for twenty years and has written fourteen books, most recently *Juarez: The Laboratory of Our Future*. He is a contributing editor of *Harper's* and *Esquire*.

Phaidon Press Limited
Regent's Wharf
All Saints Street
London N1 9PA

Phaidon Press Inc.
180 Varick Street
New York NY 10014

www.phaidon.com

First published 2001
©2001 Phaidon Press Limited

ISBN 0 7148 4025 4

Designed by Julia Hasting
Printed in Hong Kong